decompose

by S. Fey

Not a Cult
Los Angeles, CA

Edited by Shira Erlichman
Proofread by Charlotte Renner
Cover Design by Shaun Roberts

Not a Cult
Los Angeles, CA

For Nick. I stopped trying to write you poems
when I realized they were all for you.

Table of Contents

"Our sufferings do not magically end; instead we are able to wisely alchemically recycle them. They become the abundant waste that we use to make new growth possible."

—bell hooks

"There's some kind of burning inside me. It's kept me from falling apart."

—Mitski

I tell my friend, the painter, that my favorite color is orange.
He says he doesn't really believe in orange, that it's just the space
between yellow & red. He's not exactly wrong. Orange was
known in olde English as "geoluhread," meaning yellow-red. It
wasn't until the 16th century that we started calling it orange—
& even then, the color was named after the fruit, not the other
way around. He said he thought my color would be mustard,
I said *it's that too*. Carmen says my color is coral with blood.
Fitting, light with a price. I'd say my favorite color is exactly that,
the whole path from yellow to red. & haven't we always had to
make space? At home in the journey. Something wild between
primaries.

I haven't really made up a name for it yet

theory

It began with my mother, I used to have these moments often, you know, the ones where even if she couldn't do anything about it, you just wanted your mom, well, I decided it was time to have a stern talk with myself, so my self & I, we sat across from each other, my self said *now what is it you really want right now, is it your mother or is it safety, security, understanding, a warm embrace,* I let those words summer inside me before I said, yeah, a warm embrace, safety, & they said *and where's the last place you're going to get that,* eventually, I stopped crying for her, when I was honest about what I really wanted, & who couldn't give it to me—

praxis

We all contend with displacement when the rug is pulled out from underneath us, even if we pull it out ourselves, even if the rug is woven out of poison ivy, & truly, if you can use this technique with your own mother, you can use it with anyone, like for example, do I really miss you, or is it the occasional fingers running through my hair, the soothing intimacy that waltzes in & out of our atmospheres, & so the missing went away pretty quickly, there's got to be a hand out there that doesn't cost so much to hold.

Golden

After Brigit Pegeen Kelly

the last time I cried I: no
the last time I cried I harpooned
through you like a long nosed shark:
yes: I hit the shore: no: tiger pawed
sand: yes: turned back and: no
felt: felt you swim into distance
to where you came from: deep, distant
undetermined: yes: sinking, floating:
yes: whatever it was: yes:

the last time I read: no: the first
read of The Lady, or The Tiger: yes
the ending: no
   lack of ending: yes:
   lugged me to banging
      down doors
   :yes demanding the ending:

the last time I saw the ocean: yes
at sundown, I was face deep
in your thighs. we had to breathe: no:
a moment to take off our clothes: yes
we wanted each other

but in my golden gazelles I am sunrise,
where all of me begins: yes: no
end in sight

The cost of consistency

A barrel of roses. A summer fig. Honey
by the gallon. More than minimum wage
can afford. (More than I can afford). Atmospheric
layers. Right time right place. Years
of therapy. No one. Nothing. Making
your bed. A journal entry. Six new books. A window
of orchids. Honey distilled. A desire
to be yours. A full moon. 288 full moons;
forgetting your birthday. I'll forget
your birthday. It's your birthday,
I'll forget. I'll forget the full moon
today, on your birthday. It's your birthday.
I hope you're happy. Happy birthday.

You should always be gentle with yourself

you said when I accidentally scratched
my arm. This observation is astute, but

I can't think of one time you were gentle with me.

I tried. My best friend doesn't like Mario Party.
He says it's a random number generator

it doesn't matter how good you are, you may not win.

That's actually why I like it. It takes off a pressure.
I can't control the outcome, I can only play.

I gave you my best, and still didn't take home the trophy.

After I left you I used to look in the mirror and
force myself to say *today I give you my best.*

It takes seven years for your cells to regenerate. In just

four years I'll be entirely rid of you. My new trauma
therapy has made you show up in my dreams again.

One evening, I had forgiven you for rotting. That's just it

I wanted you to understand. To put thread through
needle in this story, I wanted you to say that

I was good to you. You don't really blame me.

Unclean

I hope I feel whole again come summer.
I put everything you wrote me away,
and the little knick knacks, even the rocks
you picked for me on hikes. Even the rocks.
There's a spot on the mirror where you wrote
you are perfect, which of course I erased, but after
a long shower, its shadow came for a visit. I tried
to wipe it away. No luck. You made me unclean
again. In lieu of crumbling, I cocked my head back
and said *Thanks, bro*. There will be a day
where I don't hear you in every soft melody,
man. The side of the bed you liked to sleep
on won't seem so separate to me, pal. I locked
the door between us this time. Somewhere
out there you're looking at the same sky
as me. That'll have to be enough, dude.

I'm not mad

alone

So there's two black cats a couple blocks from me by the bike path, they're a few houses down from each other & completely identical, the kind of black cats with long fur & pale green eyes, well, I swear it's actually the same black cat & they're fucking with me, makes me smile when I walk by, little trickster, & some people think black cats are unlucky, false, they're just the witchiest kind, further evidence that this is actually the same cat, my own little cheshire.

clouded

The veil is thin between fiction & real life sometimes, like this obscure sorrow I read about called *ringlorn*, the wish that the modern world felt as epic as the one depicted in old stories & folktales, like when I was tiny & would imagine I had a dragon flying in the clouds, way above me, when I was on the swingset, waiting for the right time to swoop down & rip my father's head off, like soon would be the last time he'd twist up my insides, & that's exactly why I'm not mad at you, sometimes we have to make real our own fictions, like when we're walking alone, hurting.

Wings

There's a runner and a chaser, you said, pointing at the page. *Look*. It was a book on twin flames, and all of the cycles they go through. *Well, I don't want to chase you anymore*, I said, my strength stepping out from the corner they were hiding in. If we're twin flames, then I unsubscribe. I'm good on the spiritual excuse for your bad behavior, for your foot being out the door. I'm not running after anyone, I have clothes to fold. The truth is, it doesn't matter how well I make your walnut butter. bell hooks says if you run from love's pain, you'll never know the fullness of love's pleasure. So go on, to wherever you're going, thank you for stopping by. Great wings, beautiful wings.

Dinosaur Spine

I don't know my blood type there's no direct through-line I've never seen a tree bearing my ancestry as its leaves I just know two people made me though they probably shouldn't have I say probably because I am alive and living well mystery isn't my genre if I don't know already I don't need to the good questions don't have answers and I don't ask questions I don't want the answer to I'd rather widen the lens or narrow it I don't know exactly what they did to me memory is fickle and changes to protect its keeper I don't know the pills she was taking I don't know if she was really going to kill me a voice just said run I don't know the chances of children like me surviving though I know they're mostly unforgiving I say mostly because I am alive and living well I don't know what damage was nature or nurtured I don't have the answers in theatre school they pointed it out to me the unnatural shape of my spine goddamn theatre kids and their massage trains my dinosaur spine they called it they asked *did you get hurt when you were little* yes,

A Great Nuclear Evil

2:43am

My letters & journal are rifled through & somehow I know it is by your hand. I call a useless detective to find evidence of you. You show up & proof is still inconclusive. We are in the loft of my new house, but not exactly it, & for this I will thank my subconscious. The useless man is still searching & you wrap arms around me. For one second my ribs unfurl, their wings buzz. I break you off, tell you I'm rid of you. *You'll never be done with me.*

2:45am

I wake up. A girl slides into my dms offering "sweet gifs or the blood of your enemies." I consider the blood of my enemies. Won't speak you or write you by hand. When I mouth you the air becomes poison. I'm helpless. I'm speaking of the triangular bayonet, a weapon designed to leave a hole in the shape of a triangle; a wound the body doesn't know how to heal.

Everyone calls me their husband

but no one is next to me when I wake
up from the nightmares. Briefly,
I consider the possibility of being
a third in a relationship. Not to have
sex with anyone, but to maybe hold
hands with two people who adore
me. After pondering on that more,
I realize that means I just want
parents, which, unfortunately, checks
out. Taylor says when I'm really upset
I avoid the question and make a lot
of jokes. But, Taylor, have you
seen the weather? It's raining in LA.
I've been laughing so much these days.

lesbians are exhausting

a monarch butterfly[1] soars into the jacaranda tree
i tell myself it's not a sign, it's their season
then there are two, fluttering in & out of each other
hummingbirds[2] circle me like i'm covered
in pollen the sidewalk is more like a ramp
because of tree roots that refused to be paved
over[3] hibiscus reaching through the fence
unable to be contained[4] this matcha, the same
forest as the buttons on your shirt, soft piano
from my headphones, a song i haven't skipped[5]
another hummingbird[6] climbs the tree in search
of a certain nectar, doesn't find it, leaves.
jacaranda blossoms coat the sidewalk, a purple
masterpiece[7] & why can't they just be fucking flowers

---

[1] you

[2] you

[3] you

[4] you

[5] you

[6] me

[7] you

poem in which you get to be a kid

for gaia rajan

you stub your toe, hard, you cry
& you don't. daisies open their fuzzy
bellies to you; you pollinate. chlorine trickles
nearby; the blue doesn't reach you.
you hike up the hill, you fall, & you don't.
finger paint is electricity. when you call,
blanket is your first responder. you fall asleep on the floor
somebody moves you. you swim, you splash
a great deal. somebody reads the books to you first.
nobody picks the colors of your shirts but you.
you point, & it's yours; when you speak
they listen. when your door is closed, it is closed—
if there is a faint knock; you choose. rain is just drizzle
& nobody publishes any of it.

ice cream before bed

upright

Over the cards, my friends point to "the child." New beginnings. "The crossroads." They say *there could be wrong turns*. Focus only on what's new. I inquire what a wrong turn could disguise itself as. *For example*, they say. *I know you would never. We know you would never.*

reversed

I pay for the dark chocolate waffle cone in more ways than one. This is where the muddy gets water—the dream starts with a carousel of good times. New friends on the beach, a rocky hike, & then you. I'm livid; you're back to be with me for real this time. I'm so mad as I crack my heart open again to feed you the yolk. Furious as I walk you back into my home.

Dangerous

There's this really dangerous place, it's called hell,
I'm sure you're familiar with it; people love to take you
there & call it something else. I've gotten pretty good
at figuring hell out, like for example, this time,
when it dawned on me that I had no idea what you want,
I took a really hard look around. I noticed this scratched
in message on the wall, reading *get out*, in my own
handwriting. I wish I had written it bigger, but in my defense,
I was probably very small myself. You see, I'm from here,
so you couldn't hide it from me forever. I'm not really mad
at you anymore, but I do wish you'd stop getting mail
at my house, you didn't move in, you stayed
for three weeks, that's a vacation, you don't change
your address when you go on vacation.

I can't focus right now but who can blame me?

There's no way to throw days out the window
but shouldn't I be listening to footsteps?

Poets translate intricate details & immortalize
them on the page well at least I used an ampersand.

That's another thing I'm not supposed to say "I"
this much but I need to be in I right now.

I'm just trying to keep it together &
shouldn't I be outside, listening to footsteps?

I have checked my phone twice now already how
am I ever to be an academic again?

I love my absolutes & I had breakfast with myself
today for the first time in months

'stead of the straight-from-bed-to-running
every-day-like-a-boxing-match these

days feel less like sport more
ripple in a still lake at twilight.

Logged so many hours of missing you I have to
be getting close now. I learned something

today too, my cat, she's not just scratching
the wall she's trying to climb.

Fourth Generation

I've heard—when one becomes
a parent they return to their source.
Like seeds have no choice
which plant they will bloom.

Ripped from the tree, half-ripe:
I left myself out in the sun
but the window couldn't deliver
what wasn't its responsibility.

Sometimes I imagine the canopy collect
the sky. Its roots barrel into
the soil of should-have-beens.

Then, maybe, I could pour
sweetness into a pit.

With two fingers I can squeeze the sun

From one sound to another, I would rather draw
you a diagram with shades of tea & taste
it quietly, together or not. What I'm saying
is, I'll hear it if the door closes, but sunrays
bounce off my orchid petals & cling
to each painting for dear life. I have to wonder
when they will fall. My point is, matcha
is the deepest forest. Lush. & when tasting
pine, there is so much to notice.
After 25 years, I make my bed.
Lay in it, happily, too. I'll get to my point—
I never shake the sand out of my shoes.
It swishes around so cheerfully,
am I to deny myself this?

Chicago

left

the sound of you calling my name; moonflower; foaming at the mouth; starshine; blindly romantic; sunny-faced queen; reaching for a partner, parched, fear of evaporation; cruelty without consequence; adult; deep sea diving sans oxygen tank; 922.5 days, ears pressed to your chest, tuned in to your heart, waiting for

kept

smiling in the lacking; warrior daisy; more minutes to finish the word I am spelling; architect of girl glow; hand-holder; gold-chained; smiling to sad songs; smiling because they played; dancing til 4am; sun rising from my platform

$$\frac{2}{\infty}$$

You made me feel seen exactly two times. The first:
you bought me the perfect watch. No numbers,
so it was difficult to tell the time. And wooden,
so my superstitious fist could knock on it.
The second: you couldn't sleep, so I sang to you. Just before
you nodded off, you called me an angel. A statistician
would call these outliers. This was all a big mystery
until I opened the textbook. I get it. You wanted to keep me,

you'd pay any price. I guess I had to learn the lesson
again, the first time I was too small to remember; no matter
how much I suffered you wouldn't be happy.
It would be too simple to say anything died
when I left you, except the plants. I left them outside.
You slept on a twin-sized bed, *so no one else could fit*, and glued
yourself to the wall when I joined you. I always envied
your sheets—the way you suffocated them with your form,
the way you were honest about it.

In many ways, I'm like a cornered spider

I push the wrong button and my computer
says *I can learn to understand you*
much better if I can get familiar with the way
you talk. I'm trying to waterski over the surface
now, in lieu of tying the question to a chair
and making it speak. An opening is a jar
that you can't find the lid to; now it's a glass
or recycling, but not garbage. I should have looked
for a new cabinet when I saw you throwing
glass away. You didn't like anything
unless it had a function you deemed worthy.
A perfect lid to contain itself. Dismissive
of everything but onion peels and lemon zest.
That you kept. Shaved the skin of the lemon
into tiny shards and put them in your favorite
little box in the fridge. A blue lid. I took
the little box with me when I left,
lid and all. It's really hard to waterski
for longer than minutes, but muscles
are muscles and bones are bones and they grip
and bend and carry us over the waves.

Pop

Spotify called my aura *energy & yearning*.

If you can both dance & cry to a song, it's probably up my alley.

Two years & 3,000 miles later, I remember
the way the air thickened when you first looked through my
profile.

When we were courting, we bonded over ANTI & In Rainbows.
Then you had me.

Chewed my music like it left a bad taste in your mouth.

Now when friends tie me to pop, it registers as an attack.

I accidentally let Ariana Grande make my top five artists, & she's
only the beginning.

You'll find me yelling *it's Charli, baby!*
when Charli XCX comes on & I'll never outgrow Taylor Swift.

People are surprised I love her until I remind them I was socialized
as a white girl in the suburbs.

There's an astrologer who says Stevie Nicks' Venus square Neptune
placement makes all her songs hexes that haunt her ex-boyfriends.

I don't know Taylor's chart well, but I know when a man hurt her
she had millions singing Dear John.

You remember when you cut off all your hair & I kept some of it? A joke.

I found it six months after I left.

The witches were upset when I threw it away.

Hair is a jackpot, almost as good as blood for hexes. I didn't come here to scare you.

I'm just saying, I would have felt less alone if half the world joined me in screaming your name.

I want to text you but I'm tired

of looking at screens & I hate to be negative here,
but I know how this goes: you marvel at the morsels
of sun between my fingers, I find a lucky penny
in your attention. You seem grounded—but people always do.
Even earth is shaken with a shift of plates. & you can't be dirt
to me. You can bring some though, & I'll bring
some. But my thing is, where do I get the seed?
Or what do we plant instead? I want less diagrams
& more carbonation. I want to stop mourning you
before we've met. Give me your shoelace,
anything, I'll plant it. Or—we will,

bad ideas

> *we unearth the oldest bottle only to discover*
> *we waited too long and the cork has turned to clay*
> — *Natasha Rao*

I was a terrible
idea. My mother had
me at 25, a direct
result of cheating.
In one hand, me,
in the other, gasoline
she poured all over
our lives. She didn't have
the capacity to do
the dishes in her
sink, let alone
raise a child. At 16
I ran away
for the first time,
to my narcissistic
biological father,
who at least paid
the bills on time.
At 18 I left them
all for good,
with no proof
there was anything
better out there.
Did you know
the IRS considers
playwriting a hobby?
I learned this

in my first college-
level theatre class,
and continued
to get a degree
in theatre anyway.
Two years after
I graduated, I bought
a one-way ticket
to a city I had never
been to, in the middle
of a global pandemic,
with no job lined up.
Said city had 44,000
cases of a sickness
that attacks your lungs.
I have asthma.
I have a deep desire
for a savings
account and I write
poetry. My friend,
if you find
the bottle, don't
wait. Drink.

from the body

you will get out of the water
or you will drown.
you will stretch,
if not today, tomorrow,
or you will become creaky.
&you will become it anyway

&you will become it anyway,
all of it; the gemstone, the icicle
the prey
&the one feeding.

it feels like decay,
&it is, but not in the way
you think right now.

from decay starts the cycle,
of which you know,
of which you will see so many.

you will see so many.

Are you coming home?

death

I'm thrilled about the rattle snakes. Let them multiply. Give them my address. It's the first room on the right. I'm ready for fire season. I'll breathe in deep. Get closer to the forest. I'm not close enough to the ocean. I'm talking beach-front. A mega tsunami can only reach twelve miles. Let those sea levels rise. Extra microplastics in this drink please. Where's that supervolcano when I need it? I'm here to stomp on stingrays and swim straight to the sharks. Pack it up already garbage patch. I'm hitting the road just so I have to get more gas. Southern California's the best idea I've ever had. You're leaving and this world's going with you. Bring on the fucking flood.

temperance

Show me where to soften and I'll show you where to soften. I see myself clearer in our picture. I see you clearest in liquid sunshine. When lights are absent and you fill the room instead. We wait on the side of the road for six hours and it feels like ten minutes. What do I do after you show me the piece I'm missing and leave? Yes, of course I'll drive you.

Beach day

On my first outing with the LA lesbians we roast
our toes on sun-baked sand at venice beach, right
by the rainbow lifeguard tower. Wear name
tags listing what a fellow ocean gay may need to know
about us. Name, pronouns, vaxxed or un-vaxxed,
& if you want to get a little wild, your astrological
sign. As I write libra (♎), vaxxed, they/them, I relish
providing information in pursuit of others' comfort.
All I'd like to add is my secure attachment style (92%),
that I'm not dating or looking, but that I deep-dive in friendship,
I'm a proud orchid father of six; I listen when others speak.
& if you were here, yours should say ABUSER
in red. I picture you with a group of unsuspecting queers,
gaybys, soft-hearted, tender people looking for connection.
You, grinning, wearing the costume of a good time.
Someone sweet takes your hand. Thinking you're a safe
dream, that they got lucky. The first time I consider
this, the contents of my stomach decide to split
with me. Like a good boy, I let them leave quietly.

It comes in waves

The moon controls
    more than the ocean.

        When swimming in lead,
            don't swallow.

        Watching you flip
    taught me how

Homecoming

You said I didn't listen. It's been half a decade. I still remember where you liked to study; in the union, by the piano, where occasionally someone would play. There, on the day I told you I'd like to give us a try, you said nothing, put your head on my shoulder. & the third table to the left at the undergraduate library, which is now closed, permanently. & the table on the second floor in the octagon shaped Ag building, where I would bring you dinner on your busiest day— Tuesday. Then there's the street corner where we walked on an early August afternoon, as you deconstructed the scone from that new bakery. You never liked scones, but if you were going to eat one, it'd better be flaky. & I'd listened with drums of ear & heart before I left you, when my aunt said *there are things I wanted with my whole being & twenty years later I'm so glad I didn't get them.* This wisdom played over the sound of my wanting. I starved out the flames. Which grew, hungry, so hungry, in resistance.

Bus Stop

This midwest winter, come with me to Gregory
and Dorner. The terminal wheezes
and we can listen as she too is worn thin by chilling
winds. And if ice crystals dance down to your hair,

comfy curly nest, we can travel
just a few blocks to the tropical greenhouse
conservatory. I'll trace you with mango lips, unbolt
like petals of vermillion hibiscus.

We'll write in pencil—
you can erase if you like.

Associative Amnesia

A thunderstorm, a Southern Illinois Summer. Of course
I was a little afraid. I've seen horror films. You turned
the key. Rain leaked through cracks in the green-
house, pooled on the floor. Our only light
was lightning. I have horrible night vision, your hand
lead me to the only plantless table. You only touched me
when you were drunk. Dust and dirt everywhere.
You read me a tumblr post, weeks ago, about how
people help you take your clothes off before sex
because of sex, but no one helps you
put them back on. I fumbled in the dark, after
we finished, to button one of your buttons.
What are you doing? Helping, I said. *Stop.*
You didn't hold my hand on the way out.

Edwin says I deserve to be loved with precision. I didn't understand what precision meant until I made Nick a smoothie & counted his macros in tablespoons. He says that's not precise— it's only accurate. The difference, he says, is that one tablespoon varies in weight depending on the substance, though it is, accurately, one tablespoon. If you measure in grams, 5 grams is always 5 grams. That's the difference between accurate and precise, & if you want to be consistent, you want a measurement that doesn't vary. I imagine when I'm loved with precision, I'll know the weight of it.

I'm not worried about it

We are strange. Begging to have it all
settled, and also, for perpetual change.
Have I wasted my life? asked the 26
year old to the room of people who revere
them. But have I? No really, if you kept a log
of the hours I've spent lighting my mind palace
aflame with my own hands, only to run, flailing
when I realized what the fire means. Tell me
you don't have the log? I'd be embarrassed.
Let's wipe the slate of panicked meditations
cerulean. Ignore images of me, staring up
at the ceiling, grieving the future I'd spent
the rest of the day sprinting toward. It's fine.
Anxiety hangovers are real. Does it count on
today's or yesterday's tally if I spend the morning
with a tighter neck? Weary shoulders? If I ground
my teeth in sleep, after my nightly dental hygiene routine?
They all say I'm put together. If this is put
together I think we should pull it apart.
Winny says *are you sure you're okay? I feel*
like something happened. How do I tell her
nothing happened? I didn't even leave the house.
I'm too tender for all of this. Just juice me
and give this soft magic to another warrior
to drink. I wasn't built for battle.

good

You want to be a good man, the kind that opens doors physical & metaphorical, that worships on sundays, a good man with a good hat, who tips it to his lady & says goodnight ma'am with no more than a peck on the cheek, of course; you want to build her a kitchen island, to have tea on the porch, to be a good man, crack hazelnuts for her in december & bring home each day's daily bread, bring her a colony of fish that you caught, you want to skin them, heat up the grill & throw them on, watch her pick the bones, you want her bones, you want her muscles to release, to power you like electricity, you want to build the walls to house her wire, to strip them just so, to cease sparks from flight— & like a good man, you tiptoe out of the hallway, leaving the key she made for you on the counter, & like a good man you hail a cab to the river & will never call her again, you're gone before sunrise, you wash your hands of her & dive into that river, watch wind brush its fingers through tall grass, lay back & let currents wash you over, like a good man, everything is yours.

sometimes we are wrong

At my grandfather's school they let him play
with mercury on his desk. Coca-Cola used to contain

cocaine, for a healthy hangover remedy. The Radium Girls
painted radium onto watch dials from 9-5 until the poison

ran down too many of their white blood cells. Smoking
wasn't considered an irrefutable health risk until

1956. Heroin was used as a cough suppressant. Shark
cartilage was thought to prevent cancer, even with 42

cases on record of sharks containing tumors. In the 50's,
sometime around finding out we shouldn't smoke cigarettes,

people infected themselves with tapeworms to lose
weight. In the 3rd century BC we discovered the earth is round,

but some people will still die on the hill that it's flat. & I thought
you were it.

Main Street

familiar

I know I have a crush on her when she appears in the nightmare, becomes the most important ingredient in its recipe. This place of fear and high stakes welcomes her in sinister reverence. *You're here*, I say. Like always, before this, I attempt to escape from my mother. Now, I'm walking next to my crush on a street, littered with pastel 50's cars, so stunning I hardly notice the man careening towards us, laughing maniacally. *I'm going to get you now*, he says, bashing through the curve and onto the sidewalk. Now I see it is not just any man, but my biological father. My crush is gone. I'm about to be crashed into by a man I left behind as soon as I could. I am really scared now.

blurred

I knew I could love her when I couldn't find her in the fire. In dream two, we're kissing, it feels natural, though this is the first time our mouths collide in any universe. I tell her I didn't know she liked me. *Of course I do*, she says, her hand cupping my face with a purity that's only familiar in the peach-foggy ease of dreams. Then we are not together; I walk a Scandinavian-style street. I think I recognize the building we were warm-mouthed in, but I'm not solid on that, the lucidity has begun to slip through me like sand. The buildings to my left are on fire now, and one of them is hers. I know she won't be there. Still, I call her name. As with all loves I've known, I run straight into the flames, through the door I'm most certain of.

potential

does your boyfriend know where your joy is resting
do it for you, really veins meet, yes between us
does he hold you your heart, yes do you want me to
like a little crystal where you wake it
in your palm. tick & release I could gently
know your healing yes I know. shake eyes open
potential I see it myself

Lightless

When Tor still thought he was straight, his best friend confessed his love to him. It freaked him out so bad, he fled the state. Years later, he realized he loved him right back. Went to Florida to tell him and found out he was in the ground. Tor has told me this story twice. Both times, with his head pointed to his hands. I believe feelings are meant to be shared. If something inside me knocks, I spit it out. Even if it seems impossible. My proof is this: when a lover told me to look out the window on our morning in Vegas. The strip had lost all its lights, the reckless night leaving it abandoned and bleak. She said, *It looks like regret, doesn't it?* I nodded, seeing none of myself in it.

music in the mundane

there are still notes to sing
the rolled up towels on your shelf,
meticulous melody of each tile
you scrub
orchestra of orchid petals
strewn across your altar
popular tune of when you make
that white countertop shine
instrumental order of your polished
shoes; below the hymn of your hanging
color coded wardrobe
choral pour of vinegar into the softener
dispenser, like your grandmother
showed you, rhythm
of each biweekly deep
clean— sound waves of smoothing
out your fresh sheets
you're so clean, baby, sing

Cold Turkey

I have retired from dating. My heart collects their 401k, golfs in the morning, watches their stories in the afternoon. Got a little Mr. Rogers sweater to sing *it's a beautiful day in the neighborhood*. Saturday is for poker with the boys. The superbloom meadows of peace. But if you were my wife, wouldn't we have lit the match by now? Remember the last time we waltzed at a distance. Halfway down the street, you saw the sign and said *I didn't know this was a dead end*. Me neither. On that same day, you said you didn't love me and I sparkle more than other people to you. I think that's called love, but that's enough on that for now. Listen, the lonely path is on the other line, and I'm gonna take it.

I want to lay on the couch,

but I slide on my mustard gazelles.
When I was tiny, I'd have given any good crayon
or dream to be elusive as shadow, seen only

when the light treats you right.
Now, I'd say it's so. I pick up
tiny me onto my shoulders & watch a family

teach their young to rollerblade in an empty
parking lot. Weeks ago I found three houses
with windchimes on the block to my west.

Two of them are wooden & hum
by call of breeze. My headphones make me half-
here & not listening. You only get so many

golden hour walks. Not by way of scarcity,
by way of chance. I could be scheduled
to labor right now, but I'm not, so I walk,

every day that I can. I know this little
one on my shoulders' shadow sparkles like sea-
water & today, I make sure

these late sun rays rest on them kindly.

Zora gives me a new middle name

My given middle name means bitter, which in the context of my full name, I used to like. Wise Bitter Faerie. Wise: like when I was tiny people told me I was wise beyond my years which is code for you've been asked to carry more than you can hold & nobody considered how small were your fingers. Bitter: like I used to look at the world & say cut me. I dare you. Is that what you call sharp? Reveling in just how much I could bleed & keep standing. & Faerie: which I don't have to tell you means magic. *Isaac,* Zora says. *Yes, I gave you a new middle name, do you like it?* It means one who rejoices, one who laughs. & you know what? That's Wise Laughing Faerie to you. This is my joyous era. My new challenge to this world: show me how good it can get.

write a poem about wishes

you don't have to wish on anything, actually, I like those shooting stars as much as the next guy & 11:11 is a cool time & when I blew out my birthday candles I saw shining gold, saw my current smile spread all the way into my future like raspberry jam on some good bread with real butter or if it's vegan it's miyoko's & intention holds more weight than we think, sorry if I'm falsely accusing you, if you know the weight of will like I know when milk is 140 degrees, just with the tips of my fingers & what consumes you is either wish or in the wish family, which again, is wide & old as an encyclopedia's dream, your late night yearning sends out a personal bat signal & I've been the manifestor & the manifestee, seen even the wrong wish appear right in front of me took her hand & kissed it

when you encounter the devil

After Aimee Nezhukumatathil

when you encounter the devil,
when you survive it;
you have to let it die

somewhere in you it will rot
things may grow
wrong things may grow,
too, if you water them

things will eat their way out
of you   things that crawl
out of your mouth and head first
to your truest love

when you encounter the devil;
pull the death card, peer into
its flowers   they too come
from the decompose

they decompose you, they feed
they lurch, they petal your cheek
they carve or caress;
it's up to you

when you encounter the devil,
it's up to you;

Acknowledgements

Thank you first and foremost to my orchids: Honeydew, Pear, Chicory, Basil, Plum, Eggplant, Spring Breeze, Raspberry, Apple, Lilac, Lemony Snickett, and Dragon Fruit Fey. I love you when you're blooming and when you're not.

Thank you to Daniel Lisi, Charlotte Renner, and the Not a Cult team for making this dream come true.

Thank you to my editor and teacher Shira Erlichman. You helped sculpt my craft more than any other pair of hands. You gay, wise, curious legend.

Thank you to the publications who have published poems in this book in one form or another: American Poetry Review, Poet Lore, Honey Literary, Sonora Review, The Lumiere Review, Kissing Dynamite Poetry, Ocean State Review, Voicemail Poems, manywor(l)ds place, Hooligan Magazine, Homology Lit, Knight's Library Magazine, the winnow, Indigo Literary, Kiss Your Darlings Anthology, mutiny!, The Collective Magazine, HAD, Olney Magazine, The Los Angeles Press, and Rejection Letters.

Thank you to all my Not a Cult pressmates, especially; Rhiannon McGavin, Edwin Bodney, Yesika Salgado, and Gabi Abrão for welcoming me into this not cult with open arms.

Thank you thank you thank you to my magic five: Dare Williams, Rita Mookerjee, Taylor Byas, Dia Roth, and Jason B. Crawford. You are my chosen editors, my confidants, my cheerleaders, my heartsongs. I love you I love you I love you. You held my hand every step on the way to this. Taylor, my poetry partner in all things, my first draft reader always. The most important part of my routine is to tell you "good morning." Dia, the editing love of my life. Dare, I'm your biggest fan. I love to talk to you on the phone for ten hours. Rita, you make me feel seen and fill my life with magic. Jason B., I love being poetry husbands with you.

Thank you to the poets and friends in my corner who support, challenge, nurture, and inspire me: Gaia Rajan, Natasha Rao, Susan Nguyen, KB Brookins, Vanessa Angelica Villarreal, Erin Mizrahi, Haolun Xu, Danielle P. Williams, Javier Zamora, Joey Cipriano Zamora, Taneum Bambrick, K. Iver, Joan Kwon Glass, Jess Q. Stark, Jeremy Radin, Derrick C. Brown, Meghann Pirate Plunkett, Chelsea Bayouth, Michelle Lietz, Sofía Aguilar, Mary Boo Anderson, Jeni Prater, and Aman K. Batra.

Thank you to Gem Arbogast. When I said my favorite gem is black tourmaline I lied. It's you by a landslide.

Thank you to everyone in The Luminaries poetry workshop, who believed in my work long before it became an object you could hold in your hands. Thank you to Bel, Zora, and I.S. Jones for being the wondrous friends that helped me nurture that space.

Thank you Carmen, for the endless joy our friendship brings me. "Tomorrow is always fresh with no mistakes in it."

Thank you to my family, chosen and otherwise. Thank you to my chosen parents, Erica and Robert Juenger. This book is your new grandchild. There's a hint of trying to make you proud in everything I do. To Joanne, who filled my life with a family so wonderful I couldn't possibly have dreamed it up. To my siblings: Sam, Nick, Abbie, Jordan, Keenan, Nora, and Krystyna. I carry as much as I can in the hopes of being strong enough for you.

Endless gratitude to my aunts and uncles: Aunt Margaret, Uncle Frank, Aunt Tess, Uncle Johnny, Aunt Kathy, Aunt Liz, Uncle Rich, Aunt Melissa, Uncle Scott, Uncle Chris, Aunt Jill, Aunt Mel, Uncle Hugo, Aunt Bia, Auntie Deana, Uncle Ryan, and Aunt Carrie. You make every hard day easier, and rest underneath any fear I have like a safety net waiting to catch me.

Thank you to my grandparents: Grandpa Ed, Grandma Ardy, Grandpa Ted, Shotzi, Nana, and Nance.

Thank you to Penny and Samuel, my niece and nephew. Here's to hoping you think I'm cool when you're old enough to read this. Thank you to Cole for bringing them into this world.

Thank you to Barry Fey, my style icon, for never letting me win at any games when I was small. I credit you for my optimistic and relentless acceptance of a challenge. Thank you Uncle Nathan, for being a wise and nurturing light.

Thank you to Aunt Kristin, Courtney, and Uncle Brian. I love being a family of four with you.

Thank you to Kerry, the greatest Unmother there ever was.

Thank you to Molly Noel, Patrick Green, Mark Lard, Bridget Sundeen, and all the other guardian angels that got me through the first 18 years of my life. Thank you to Valerie and Martie for taking me in when I needed it.

Thank you to my big LA family: Jeremy, David, Winny, Charlie, Al, Thoughts, Melissa, Jim, and Xavier. I've been waiting for a creative community like you my whole life. And to Brian, who never lets me cancel the Sun, ever opening my shades to let in the light. Lily, for dancing around the living room with me. Stasia, for being 90% of my phone log and the biggest blessing. Tito, you make every moment we share into music. James, my filmmaking partner, my subconscious was loud when you handed me a golden ticket in my dream. Faria, mother to us all, Aquarius Queen of my world. Jenny, for our new moon rituals and for always seeing me. Emmylou, my writing partner who refuses to let me quit theatre. May we always plague each other with more projects.

Thank you to my friends, you have contributed to my work more than you know. You make my life full and distract me with fun when I should be writing: Cassi, Allen, Jules, Jesse, Alexis, Mari, Jola, Kathy, Julieta, Jon, Netta, Gregory, Matt, Vanessa, Lily, Sherry, Jess, Ian, Kelly, Yvon, Rachel, Claire, Jena, Lauren, Morgan, Alexa, Shaleigh, Chelsea, Elias, Liz, Jack, Brittany, and Michael.

Thank you to Young and Caffe Paradiso.

Thank you to JW, Thom, Latrelle, Peter Davis, Valleri, and Anderson for the support and guidance at a very pivotal time in my life. I remind myself of your teachings every day.

Thank you to the late Michael David Madonick, who read the very first version of this book eight years ago. You live in these pages.

Thank you to Sofia and George. The safest place. The Universe knew what they were doing when we all became baristas on the same day.

Thank you to Maddie Terlap. I wouldn't be here without you, you fool.

Finally, thank you to Nick. My platonic life partner. My life found its track when I met you.

S. Fey is a Queer and Trans writer living in LA. Currently, they are the poetry editor at Hooligan Magazine, and co creative director at Rock Pocket Productions. Their work has appeared in American Poetry Review, Poet Lore, The Sonora Review, and others. They love to beat their friends at Mario Party. They tweet @sfeycreates. Photo Credit: Brian Seungheon Kim.

Printed in the USA
CPSIA information can be obtained
at www.ICGtesting.com
JSHW022346200324
59605JS00005B/6